Navigating Gender: A Guide for Parents of Gender Nonconforming Children

Copyright Page

TITLE: Navigating Gender: A Guide for Parents of Gender Nonconforming Children

1ST Edition

Copyright @ 2023

Roberto M. Rodriguez. All rights reserved.

ISBN: 9798223940845

Table of Contents

Navigating Gender: A Guide for Parents of Gender Nonconforming Children

By Roberto Miguel Rodriguez

Chapter 1: Understanding Gender Identity

The Spectrum of Gender

Understanding the spectrum of gender is crucial for parents navigating the complexities of raising gender nonconforming individuals. In today's society, gender is no longer confined to the binary construct of male and female. Instead, it encompasses a wide range of identities and expressions that exist on the spectrum of gender.

At one end of the spectrum are individuals who are born with an undefined sex at birth. These individuals may have physical characteristics that do not fit neatly into the traditional categories of male or female. Understanding and accepting the uniqueness of their child's identity is essential for parents in this situation.

Gender nonconforming individuals are those who do not conform to societal expectations and norms associated with their assigned gender at birth. These individuals may express themselves in ways that challenge traditional gender roles and stereotypes. It is crucial for parents to support and validate their child's identity, creating a safe and accepting environment.

Intersex individuals are born with physical attributes that do not align with typical male or female characteristics. They may have a combination of both male and female biological traits. Parents of intersex children should educate themselves about intersexuality, seek medical advice from experts, and ensure their child's well-being and mental health.

Non-binary individuals do not identify exclusively as male or female. They may identify as a combination of both genders or as a gender outside of the binary spectrum altogether. Parents should respect their child's pronoun preferences and provide them with the necessary support to navigate a world that often fails to recognize non-binary identities.

Transgender individuals are individuals whose gender identity does not align with their assigned sex at birth. They may transition to align their physical appearance with their true gender identity. Parents should educate themselves about transgender experiences, provide emotional support, and advocate for their child's rights and well-being.

Genderqueer, genderfluid, agender, bigender, two-spirit, and androgynous individuals are all unique identities that fall under the umbrella of the gender spectrum. It is essential for parents to listen to their child's self-identification and provide the necessary support and understanding.

Navigating the spectrum of gender can be challenging for parents, but it is essential to remember that every individual's experience is valid and deserves respect. By educating themselves, seeking support from relevant communities, and providing a nurturing and accepting environment, parents can ensure their gender nonconforming child thrives and feels loved for who they truly are. Remember, your child's identity is a beautiful part of their uniqueness, and embracing it will lead to their happiness and self-fulfillment.

Exploring Gender Identity

Understanding gender identity is an essential step for parents of gender nonconforming individuals. In this subchapter, we will delve into the complexities of gender, providing insights and guidance to parents who are navigating this unique journey with their children. We will discuss various aspects of gender identity, including the undefined sex at birth, gender nonconforming individuals, intersex individuals, non-binary individuals, transgender individuals, genderqueer individuals, genderfluid individuals, agender individuals, bigender individuals, two-spirit individuals, and androgynous individuals.

The undefined sex at birth refers to cases where the biological sex of a child cannot be clearly determined at birth. This can be a challenging situation for parents, as they may struggle to assign a gender to their child. We will explore how parents can create a supportive environment that respects their child's individuality and allows them the freedom to explore their gender identity.

Gender nonconforming individuals are those who express themselves in ways that do not align with traditional gender expectations. We will provide parents with strategies to support their gender nonconforming children, helping them navigate societal pressures and fostering a sense of self-acceptance.

Intersex individuals are born with physical characteristics that do not fit typical binary definitions of male or female. We will discuss the unique challenges faced by intersex individuals and provide resources for parents to educate themselves and advocate for their child's rights.

Non-binary individuals identify outside of the traditional gender binary, rejecting the categorization of male or female. We will explore the experiences of non-binary individuals and offer guidance to parents on how best to support and affirm their child's gender identity.

Transgender individuals experience a disconnect between their gender identity and the sex assigned at birth. We will address common concerns parents may have and provide tools to help them navigate the emotional and practical aspects of supporting their transgender child.

In addition to the aforementioned identities, we will also touch on genderqueer, genderfluid, agender, bigender, two-spirit, and androgynous individuals. By exploring these diverse gender identities, parents can gain a deeper understanding of the spectrum of gender and provide a nurturing environment for their children.

Throughout this subchapter, we will emphasize the importance of open communication, empathy, and unconditional love. By embracing and celebrating their child's gender identity, parents can empower them to live authentically and thrive in a world that often misunderstands and marginalizes gender nonconforming individuals.

Navigating gender identity is a continuous journey, and this subchapter aims to equip parents with the knowledge and tools needed to support their gender nonconforming child every step of the way. Together, we can create a more inclusive and accepting world for all individuals, regardless of their gender identity.

The Importance of Supporting Gender Nonconforming Individuals

In today's rapidly evolving society, it is crucial for parents to understand and support their gender nonconforming children. This subchapter aims to shed light on the significance of embracing and advocating for individuals who do not conform to traditional gender norms. By doing so, parents can foster an environment of acceptance, love, and understanding, ensuring their child's emotional well-being and overall happiness.

The Undefined Sex at Birth

For parents whose child's sex is undefined at birth, it is imperative to create a space where their child can freely explore and express their gender identity. By providing a nurturing environment that allows for self-discovery, parents can help their child navigate the complexities of gender with confidence and assurance.

Gender Nonconforming Individuals

Gender nonconforming individuals may express themselves in ways that defy society's expectations of masculinity or femininity. As parents, it is crucial to acknowledge and validate their child's gender expression, as it plays a significant role in their identity formation. By embracing their child's unique expression, parents can instill a sense of self-acceptance, empowering their child to love themselves for who they truly are.

Intersex Individuals

Intersex individuals are born with physical characteristics that do not fit typical definitions of male or female. Parents of intersex children must prioritize informed decision-making and consent, ensuring that the child's bodily autonomy and emotional well-being are protected. By seeking support from experts and connecting with intersex communities, parents can navigate the challenges and advocate for their child's rights effectively.

Non-binary, Transgender, Genderqueer, Genderfluid, Agender, Bigender, Two-spirit, Androgynous Individuals

These identities fall under the umbrella of gender nonconformity. Parents must educate themselves about these experiences, terminologies, and challenges their children may face. By actively supporting their child's authentic gender identity, parents can create a safe and loving environment that fosters self-discovery and self-acceptance.

In conclusion, supporting gender nonconforming individuals is of utmost importance for parents. By embracing their child's unique identity, parents can cultivate an atmosphere of love, acceptance, and understanding. This subchapter aims to equip parents with the knowledge and tools necessary to navigate the complexities of gender nonconformity, ensuring their child's emotional well-being and affirming their right to be themselves. It is through this support that parents can empower their children to confidently navigate their own gender journeys with pride.

Chapter 2: The Undefined Sex at Birth

Understanding Intersexuality

Intersexuality is a topic that is often misunderstood and overlooked in discussions about gender. In this subchapter, we will explore the concept of intersexuality and its significance for parents of gender nonconforming individuals. Understanding intersexuality is crucial for creating a supportive and inclusive environment for all children, regardless of their assigned sex at birth.

Intersex individuals are born with biological variations in their sex characteristics that do not fit typical definitions of male or female. These variations can manifest in various ways, such as differences in chromosomes, hormones, or reproductive organs. It is estimated that intersex traits occur in approximately 1 in 2,000 births, highlighting the importance of recognizing and understanding this diverse population.

For parents of gender nonconforming individuals, it is essential to recognize that gender identity and intersexuality are distinct concepts. While gender identity relates to one's internal sense of being male, female, or nonbinary, intersexuality refers to the physical characteristics of an individual's sex. It is possible for a person to be both intersex and identify as any gender.

Understanding intersexuality helps parents navigate the complexities their children may face. Intersex individuals often encounter challenges related to disclosure, medical interventions, and societal expectations. As a parent, being knowledgeable about intersexuality allows you to advocate for your child's rights and well-being.

To support your child, it is crucial to create an open and non-judgmental environment where they feel comfortable discussing their feelings, concerns, and experiences. Encourage conversations about intersexuality, highlighting the importance of self-acceptance and embracing diversity. Educating yourself and your child about different intersex variations and medical interventions will also empower you to make informed decisions and challenge any discriminatory practices.

Additionally, it is vital to connect with support networks and organizations dedicated to intersex rights and advocacy. These resources can offer guidance, information, and a sense of community. Remember that you are not alone in this journey, and there are others who have navigated similar challenges.

Understanding intersexuality is a journey that requires ongoing education and empathy. By embracing the diversity of sex characteristics and challenging societal norms, parents can create an inclusive and affirming environment for their gender nonconforming children. Together, we can foster a world that celebrates and respects the rich tapestry of human experiences, including intersexuality.

Challenges Faced by Intersex Individuals

Intersex individuals, those born with variations in their physical sex characteristics, face unique challenges in a society that often adheres strictly to binary gender norms. As parents of gender nonconforming individuals, it is crucial to understand and empathize with the specific obstacles intersex individuals may encounter throughout their lives.

One of the primary challenges faced by intersex individuals is societal misunderstanding and ignorance. Many people lack awareness and knowledge about intersex variations, leading to misconceptions, stigma, and discrimination. It is essential for parents to educate themselves about intersexuality, so they can support and advocate for their intersex child effectively.

Medical interventions and surgeries are another significant challenge faced by intersex individuals. Historically, doctors have often recommended and performed unnecessary surgeries on intersex infants to conform their bodies to societal expectations. These procedures can have long-lasting physical and psychological consequences, causing distress and robbing intersex individuals of their autonomy and bodily integrity. Parents should be aware of these potential interventions and seek informed medical advice before making any decisions regarding their child's care.

Intersex individuals often struggle with their gender identity and finding a sense of belonging within the gender binary construct. They may experience confusion, isolation, and a lack of acceptance from both their families and society at large. Parents can play a crucial role in supporting their intersex child by creating a safe and inclusive environment where they can explore and express their gender identity freely.

Another challenge faced by intersex individuals is the legal system, which often fails to recognize and protect their rights. Many countries still require individuals to have a binary sex designation on legal documents, which can be distressing for intersex individuals who do not conform to the traditional male or female categories. Parents can advocate for legal reform and encourage their intersex child to be proud of their unique identity.

In conclusion, intersex individuals face numerous challenges due to societal ignorance, medical interventions, gender identity struggles, and legal barriers. As parents of gender nonconforming individuals, it is crucial to educate ourselves about intersexuality, provide a supportive environment, and advocate for the rights and well-being of our intersex children. By doing so, we can help them navigate the challenges they may encounter and ensure they feel loved, accepted, and valued for who they are.

Nurturing a Positive Identity for Intersex Children

Introduction:

In this subchapter, we will explore the importance of nurturing a positive identity for intersex children. Intersex individuals are born with biological variations that do not fit typical male or female categories. As parents, it is crucial to create an environment that celebrates and supports their unique gender identity. By understanding the challenges intersex children may face, we can guide them towards self-acceptance and help them navigate their gender journey with confidence.

1. Embracing Diversity:

Parents of intersex children must first acknowledge and embrace the diversity within the gender spectrum. Recognizing that gender is not limited to a binary framework is essential. By creating a safe and inclusive space, you can help your child understand that their identity is valid and worthy of celebration.

2. Open and Honest Communication:

Communication is key in nurturing a positive identity for intersex children. Engage in open conversations about their feelings and experiences surrounding their gender. Encourage them to express themselves freely, without fear of judgment. By listening attentively, you can provide emotional support and validate their experiences.

3. Educate Yourself:

As parents, it is important to educate yourself about intersex variations, medical interventions, and the potential challenges your child might face. Understanding the terminology, medical procedures, and legal rights will empower you to advocate for your child effectively. Seek out resources, support groups, and professionals who specialize in intersex issues to gain knowledge and guidance.

4. Support Networks:

Building a support network is crucial for both you and your child. Connect with other parents of intersex children, gender nonconforming individuals, and the various niches within the gender spectrum. Sharing experiences, resources, and insights can provide invaluable support, guidance, and a sense of community.

5. Empower Your Child:

Encourage your child to explore and embrace their unique identity. Help them discover and express their interests, talents, and passions. Encouraging them to participate in activities that promote self-confidence and self-expression, such as art or sports, can foster a positive sense of self.

6. Professional Support:

Seeking professional support from therapists, counselors, or gender specialists who are knowledgeable about intersex issues can be immensely beneficial. These professionals can offer guidance, help your child navigate any challenges they may face, and provide a safe space for them to express their emotions.

Conclusion:

Nurturing a positive identity for intersex children requires love, acceptance, and understanding. By embracing diversity, engaging in open communication, educating yourself, building support networks, empowering your child, and seeking professional guidance, you can create an environment where your intersex child can thrive and develop a strong sense of self. Remember, your role as a parent is to support, advocate, and celebrate your child's unique gender journey.

Chapter 3: Gender Nonconforming Individuals

Defining Gender Nonconformity

In order to better understand and support our gender nonconforming children, it is essential for parents to have a clear understanding of what gender nonconformity means. This subchapter aims to provide a comprehensive definition of gender nonconformity and its various manifestations, catering to the unique needs of our diverse audience, including parents of The Undefined Sex at Birth, Gender nonconforming individuals, Intersex individuals, Non-binary individuals, Transgender individuals, Genderqueer individuals, Genderfluid individuals, Agender individuals, Bigender individuals, Two-spirit individuals, and Androgynous individuals.

Gender nonconformity refers to a person's expression, behavior, or identity that does not align with society's expectations or norms associated with their assigned sex at birth. It encompasses a broad range of experiences, feelings, and identities, and can manifest in different ways for different individuals. It is important to note that gender nonconformity is not limited to a specific gender identity or sexual orientation – it is a unique aspect of one's individuality.

For some individuals, gender nonconformity may be evident in their clothing choices, hairstyles, or interests that are typically associated with the opposite gender. Others may express their gender nonconformity through their preferred pronouns, or by rejecting traditional gender roles and stereotypes. Gender nonconforming individuals may also experience discomfort or dysphoria with their assigned gender, indicating a possible need for further exploration of their gender identity.

It is crucial for parents to remember that gender nonconformity is not a phase or a choice; it is an inherent aspect of our children's identities. By embracing and supporting their gender nonconforming child, parents can create a safe and nurturing environment where their child can thrive and develop a positive self-image.

Understanding the various terms associated with gender nonconformity is also important. Intersex individuals are born with physical characteristics that do not fit typical male or female categories. Non-binary individuals identify outside the traditional gender binary of male or female. Transgender individuals identify with a gender different from the one assigned at birth. Meanwhile, genderqueer, genderfluid, agender, bigender, two-spirit, and androgynous individuals may have unique expressions, identities, or combinations of genders that transcend the binary system.

By familiarizing ourselves with these terms and concepts, parents can better support their gender nonconforming child on their journey of self-discovery and affirmation. Through education, empathy, and open communication, we can foster a society that celebrates and respects the diversity of gender identities and expressions.

In the following chapters, we will delve deeper into the personal experiences of gender nonconforming individuals and provide practical guidance for parents navigating this complex terrain. Together, we can create a world where all children can flourish and be celebrated for their authentic selves.

Challenges Faced by Gender Nonconforming Individuals

In this subchapter, we will explore the various challenges that gender nonconforming individuals face on a daily basis. Understanding these challenges is crucial for parents who are navigating the journey of raising a gender nonconforming child or supporting their gender nonconforming loved one.

The Undefined Sex at Birth

One of the challenges faced by gender nonconforming individuals is the societal expectation of assigning a binary sex to every newborn. This can create confusion and pressure for those who do not fit neatly into the traditional categories of male or female.

Gender nonconforming individuals

Gender nonconforming individuals often find themselves challenging societal norms and expectations. They may face discrimination, misunderstanding, and even rejection from friends, family, and society at large. Parents can play a vital role in providing a supportive and accepting environment for their gender nonconforming child.

Intersex individuals

Intersex individuals are born with physical attributes that do not fit typical definitions of male or female. They face unique challenges, including medical interventions, societal stigma, and navigating their own gender identity. Parents can educate themselves about intersexuality and advocate for their child's rights and well-being.

Non-binary individuals

Non-binary individuals identify outside the traditional gender binary of male or female. They often face challenges such as being misgendered, invalidated, or erased. Parents can support their non-binary child by using their preferred pronouns, educating others, and creating inclusive spaces at home and in their communities.

Transgender individuals

Transgender individuals experience a disconnect between their gender identity and the sex assigned to them at birth. They face significant challenges, including discrimination, limited access to healthcare, and legal hurdles. Parents can provide emotional support, advocate for their child's rights, and seek resources to help navigate their child's transition.

Genderqueer, Genderfluid, Agender, Bigender, Two-spirit, Androgynous individuals

Individuals who identify as genderqueer, genderfluid, agender, bigender, two-spirit, or androgynous face unique challenges that vary across individuals. They often struggle with societal expectations, finding acceptance, and understanding their own identities. Parents can actively listen, validate their child's experiences, and seek support from communities and organizations specializing in gender diversity.

In conclusion, gender nonconforming individuals face a range of challenges in various aspects of their lives. As parents, it is crucial to educate ourselves, provide support, and create safe and inclusive spaces for our gender nonconforming children. By understanding the challenges they face, we can better advocate for their rights, ensure their well-being, and foster a sense of belonging in a society that is still learning to embrace gender diversity.

Creating a Safe and Supportive Environment

In this subchapter, we will delve into the importance of creating a safe and supportive environment for gender nonconforming individuals, specifically those whose sex at birth is undefined. As parents, your role in providing a nurturing space for your child is crucial for their emotional well-being and self-acceptance.

Understanding that your child may not conform to societal gender norms is the first step towards creating a safe environment. It is essential to educate yourself about the complexities of gender identity and the unique experiences that your child may face. By gaining knowledge and awareness, you can better empathize with your child and support them in their journey.

Communication plays a vital role in establishing a safe and supportive environment. Encourage open and honest conversations with your child about their feelings, concerns, and experiences. Be an active listener and validate their emotions, reassuring them that their thoughts and experiences are valid and important. Providing a safe space for them to express themselves without judgment will foster trust and strengthen your relationship.

Creating an inclusive home environment is also crucial. Consider incorporating gender-neutral language, allowing your child to explore different interests and hobbies without attaching gender stereotypes, and providing them with a variety of toys, books, and media that reflect diverse gender identities. This will help your child feel accepted and valued for who they are, rather than being confined by societal expectations.

It is essential to advocate for your child's rights and well-being outside of the home as well. Educate your family members, friends, and your child's school community about gender diversity, challenging harmful stereotypes and promoting inclusivity. By doing so, you are creating a network of support that will help your child navigate through any challenges they may encounter.

Lastly, remember to prioritize self-care for yourself as a parent. Navigating your child's gender journey can be emotionally challenging at times. Seek support from other parents, therapists, or support groups who understand and can provide guidance. By taking care of yourself, you will be better equipped to provide the love and support your child needs.

Creating a safe and supportive environment for gender nonconforming individuals with an undefined sex at birth requires education, open communication, inclusivity, advocacy, and self-care. By implementing these strategies, you are fostering an environment where your child can thrive, grow, and embrace their true selves.

Chapter 4: Non-binary Individuals

Understanding Non-binary Identity

In today's evolving society, traditional concepts of gender are being challenged and expanded. As parents, it is essential to educate ourselves about the various gender identities that exist to support our gender nonconforming children. One such identity is non-binary, also known as genderqueer or gender nonconforming.

Non-binary individuals identify outside of the binary gender system of male and female. They may feel that they don't fully align with either gender or that their gender identity fluctuates over time. It is crucial to understand that non-binary identity is not a phase or a trend but a valid and authentic expression of one's self.

The journey to understanding non-binary identity starts with acceptance and open-mindedness. It is natural to have questions or concerns when our children express their non-binary identity, but it is essential to approach these conversations with empathy and respect. By actively listening to our children, we can learn about their unique experiences and perspectives.

One common misconception about non-binary identity is that it is solely about gender expression or presentation. While gender expression can be a part of one's identity, non-binary individuals often experience a deep sense of disconnect from the traditional binary understanding of gender. They may use pronouns such as they/them instead of he/him or she/her, which reflects their gender identity more accurately.

It is crucial to create a safe and inclusive environment where our children can explore their non-binary identity freely. Educating ourselves about non-binary experiences and terminologies can help us support and advocate for our children effectively. By using their preferred pronouns, respecting their chosen names, and acknowledging their gender identity, we validate their sense of self.

Navigating the undefined sex at birth can be particularly challenging for parents. The traditional understanding of gender revolves around the assumption of binary sex assigned at birth. However, non-binary individuals may not fit neatly into the male or female categories. It is essential to remember that gender identity is not determined by physical attributes but by an individual's internal sense of self.

As parents, we play a crucial role in normalizing non-binary identities and challenging societal norms. By educating ourselves and advocating for our children, we can create a supportive environment that fosters their self-discovery and self-acceptance. Understanding non-binary identity is an ongoing process, but by embracing our children's authentic selves, we can help them thrive and navigate the complexities of gender with confidence.

Supporting Non-binary Children and Teens

In this subchapter, we will explore the essential aspects of supporting non-binary children and teens, providing guidance and resources for parents navigating the journey alongside their gender nonconforming child. Understanding and supporting children who identify outside the traditional gender binary is crucial for their well-being and self-acceptance.

When parents discover that their child is non-binary, they may experience a range of emotions, including confusion, concern, and even fear. However, it is important to approach this revelation with an open mind and a willingness to learn. By creating a safe and accepting environment, parents can foster their child's self-confidence and validate their gender identity.

One crucial aspect of supporting non-binary children and teens is using the correct pronouns. It is essential to respect their chosen pronouns, whether it's they/them, ze/zir, or any other gender-neutral pronouns. Make a conscious effort to use the correct pronouns consistently, both at home and in public, to demonstrate your acceptance and support.

Educating yourself about non-binary identities is also crucial. Take the time to read books, attend workshops, or join support groups to gain a deeper understanding of the experiences and challenges faced by non-binary individuals. This knowledge will help you provide informed support and serve as a knowledgeable advocate for your child.

Communication is key when it comes to supporting non-binary children and teens. Encourage open and honest conversations with your child, allowing them to express their thoughts, feelings, and concerns freely. Actively listen and validate their experiences, ensuring they feel heard and understood. Additionally, maintain an ongoing dialogue about their gender identity, as it may evolve over time.

Building a supportive community is essential for both parents and their non-binary children. Seek out local or online support groups where parents can connect with others who share similar experiences. These groups can provide a safe space to share stories, exchange advice, and find emotional support.

Lastly, remember that every non-binary child's journey is unique. While some may express a desire to transition socially or medically, others may not. Allow your child to explore their gender identity at their own pace, without imposing expectations or limitations. Unconditional love, acceptance, and support are the greatest gifts parents can give to their non-binary children and teens.

By embracing these strategies and learning from the experiences of other parents and gender nonconforming individuals, parents can navigate the challenges and uncertainties of raising non-binary children and teens. Together, we can create a world that celebrates and supports all gender identities, ensuring a brighter, more inclusive future for our children.

Encouraging Self-Expression and Authenticity

In today's rapidly evolving world, gender norms and expectations are being challenged, and it is essential for parents to support and encourage their gender nonconforming children in their journey of self-expression and authenticity. This subchapter aims to provide guidance to parents of gender nonconforming individuals, particularly those who are born with an undefined sex.

Understanding that the sex assigned at birth may not align with a child's gender identity is the first step for parents. It is crucial to create an open and accepting environment where your child feels safe to express themselves authentically. Encouraging self-expression can be as simple as allowing your child to choose their preferred clothing, hairstyles, and hobbies, regardless of societal gender norms. This will help them develop a sense of identity and boost their self-confidence.

Listening and communicating effectively with your child is vital. Create opportunities for open discussions about gender identity and expression. Show genuine interest in learning about their experiences and feelings. By actively listening and validating their emotions, you demonstrate your unconditional love and support. Remember, your child's gender identity is not a phase or a choice – it is an integral part of who they are.

Educating yourself about gender diversity is equally important. Seek out resources, books, and support groups that provide valuable insights into the experiences of gender nonconforming individuals. By educating yourself, you will be better equipped to support and advocate for your child. Additionally, connecting with other parents of gender nonconforming children can provide a sense of community and reassurance.

Encouraging self-expression and authenticity also involves challenging societal prejudices and stereotypes. Help your child understand that they are not alone and that there is a whole community of individuals who embrace their identity. Celebrate and affirm their uniqueness, emphasizing that their worth is not defined by conformity to societal expectations.

Finally, be patient and understanding. Your child's journey of self-discovery and self-acceptance may take time. Offer them unconditional love, support, and acceptance throughout their exploration, and let them know that you are there for them every step of the way.

By encouraging self-expression and authenticity in your gender nonconforming child, you empower them to live a fulfilling and happy life while dismantling societal gender norms. Remember, your unwavering support can make all the difference in their journey of self-discovery and self-acceptance.

Chapter 5: Transgender Individuals

Understanding Transgender Identity

In this subchapter, we delve into the complex and often misunderstood topic of transgender identity. As parents, it is crucial for us to educate ourselves and gain a deeper understanding of this aspect of gender nonconformity in order to provide the necessary support and guidance for our children who may be questioning their gender identity.

Transgender individuals are those whose gender identity does not align with the sex they were assigned at birth. While sex is typically determined by physical characteristics such as genitalia, gender identity is a deeply personal and innate sense of being male, female, or something else entirely. It is important to recognize that gender identity is not a choice but an integral part of a person's identity.

Many parents may have questions about how to determine if their child is transgender. It is crucial to remember that only the individual themselves can truly know their gender identity. It is our role as parents to create a safe and supportive environment for our children to explore their gender identity and express themselves authentically.

It is also important to understand that transgender individuals may choose to transition, a process that aligns their physical appearance with their gender identity. Transitioning can involve various steps such as hormone therapy, surgeries, and changes in presentation, all of which should be approached with respect and support. It is crucial for parents to provide emotional support throughout this process, as it can be challenging for transgender individuals to face societal prejudice and discrimination.

As parents of children who may have been assigned an undefined sex at birth, it is even more vital to approach the topic of transgender identity with an open mind and a willingness to learn. By seeking knowledge and understanding, we can become better equipped to support our children on their journey of self-discovery and self-acceptance.

Throughout this subchapter, we will explore various aspects of transgender identity, including the challenges faced by transgender individuals, the importance of using correct pronouns, and the potential mental health implications. We will also provide resources for parents to further educate themselves and seek support from professionals and support groups specialized in transgender issues.

By understanding transgender identity, we can create a loving and accepting environment for our children, fostering their emotional well-being and helping them navigate the complexities of gender nonconformity with confidence and resilience.

Navigating Gender Transitions

Understanding and supporting your child's gender journey can be a challenging and emotional experience for parents. In this subchapter, we will explore the intricacies of gender transitions and provide guidance on how you can best support your gender nonconforming child through this transformative process.

The Undefined Sex at Birth

For parents of children with an undefined sex at birth, the journey towards discovering their child's true gender identity can be particularly complex. It is essential to approach this process with an open mind, empathy, and a willingness to learn.

The first step is to educate yourself about the various aspects of gender identity and expression. Understanding that gender is not solely determined by biological sex at birth is crucial. Your child's gender identity may differ from the assumptions made based on their physical appearance, and it is vital to respect and affirm their authentic self.

Communication is key when navigating gender transitions. Initiate open and honest conversations with your child to express your support and willingness to learn and understand. Allow them to share their experiences and emotions, and validate their feelings throughout the process. This open line of communication will foster trust and help you better comprehend their needs.

Seeking professional guidance from therapists or gender specialists can also be beneficial during this time. They can provide you with the necessary tools to navigate this journey and help you understand the emotional and psychological aspects of your child's gender transition.

It is important to create a safe and inclusive environment for your child at home. Respect their pronouns and chosen name, and educate other family members and friends about the importance of using the correct gender-affirming language. Encourage your child to express themselves authentically and support their exploration of gender expression.

Navigating gender transitions may involve various steps, such as social transition, medical intervention, or legal changes. Each person's journey is unique, and supporting your child through these steps requires patience, understanding, and unconditional love.

Remember, your child's gender journey is not a reflection of your parenting or their upbringing. By embracing their authentic self, you are providing them with the love and support they need to thrive.

In conclusion, navigating gender transitions for parents of gender nonconforming individuals with an undefined sex at birth can be a complex and emotional process. Educating yourself, fostering open communication, seeking professional guidance, creating a safe environment, and offering unconditional love are essential steps towards supporting your child's gender journey. By doing so, you become an invaluable ally in their path towards self-discovery, self-acceptance, and living their truth.

Advocating for Transgender Rights and Inclusion

In this subchapter, we will discuss the importance of advocating for transgender rights and inclusion in society. As parents of gender nonconforming individuals, it is crucial to understand the challenges faced by transgender individuals and actively work towards creating a more inclusive and accepting world for them.

Transgender rights encompass a range of issues, including legal protections, healthcare access, employment opportunities, and education. By advocating for these rights, we can help ensure that our children have equal opportunities and are treated with dignity and respect. Here are some key points to consider when advocating for transgender rights:

1. Education and Awareness: It is important to educate ourselves about transgender issues and terminology to better understand our child's experiences. By staying informed, we can challenge misconceptions and promote acceptance within our communities.

2. Support and Empathy: As parents, it is essential to provide a safe and supportive environment for our gender nonconforming children. By listening to their needs and concerns, we can be their strongest advocates and allies.

3. Affirming Language: Using affirming language is vital in creating an inclusive environment. This includes using preferred pronouns and names, as well as avoiding derogatory or offensive terms. By modeling respectful language, we can encourage others to do the same.

4. Community Engagement: Engaging with local LGBTQ+ organizations and support groups can provide valuable resources and networks. By actively participating in these communities, we can contribute to collective efforts for transgender rights and inclusion.

5. Legislative Advocacy: Contacting elected officials and advocating for transgender-inclusive policies is crucial for effecting systemic change. By supporting legislation that protects transgender individuals from discrimination, we can contribute to a more equitable society.

6. Celebrating Diversity: Promoting visibility and celebrating the achievements and contributions of transgender individuals helps challenge stereotypes and foster inclusion. By recognizing and appreciating diverse gender identities, we can help create a more accepting society for all.

By advocating for transgender rights and inclusion, we are not only supporting our own children but also creating a more inclusive world for future generations. It is essential to remember that our advocacy is not just limited to our immediate families but extends to the broader community. Together, we can make a difference and navigate the complexities of gender with compassion, understanding, and a commitment to equality.

Chapter 6: Genderqueer Individuals

Defining Genderqueer Identity

In this subchapter, we delve into the complex and diverse world of genderqueer identity. For parents of gender nonconforming individuals, understanding and supporting their child's unique journey is of utmost importance. The term "genderqueer" is often used to describe individuals who do not conform to traditional binary notions of gender, and it encompasses a wide range of identities and experiences.

Genderqueer individuals may identify as both, neither, or a combination of male and female genders. They may also identify as nonbinary, genderfluid, or agender, among other terms. This fluidity challenges the conventional understanding of gender as a fixed and binary concept. It is crucial for parents to recognize that these identities are valid and deserve respect and acceptance.

One important aspect of understanding genderqueer identity is recognizing the distinction between gender identity and sexual orientation. Gender identity refers to an individual's internal sense of their own gender, while sexual orientation refers to whom a person is attracted to emotionally, romantically, or sexually. It is essential to avoid assuming a genderqueer individual's sexual orientation based on their gender identity.

Navigating genderqueer identity can be a complex journey for both the individual and their parents. Parents play a vital role in providing support and creating a safe and affirming environment for their child. Open and honest communication is key, as it allows parents to understand their child's experiences, concerns, and needs.

Educating oneself about genderqueer identities and seeking resources such as support groups, books, and online communities can be immensely helpful. These resources can provide valuable insights into the experiences of genderqueer individuals and offer guidance on how to support and advocate for them.

It is crucial for parents to validate and respect their child's chosen name, pronouns, and gender expression. By doing so, parents demonstrate their unwavering support and love. It is also important to be patient and understanding, as a genderqueer individual's identity may evolve over time.

As parents, it is normal to have questions and concerns. Seeking professional guidance from therapists or counselors who specialize in gender identity can provide valuable support for both parents and their child. These professionals can help navigate the complexities of genderqueer identity and offer strategies for fostering a healthy and inclusive family dynamic.

In conclusion, understanding and embracing genderqueer identity is essential for parents of gender nonconforming individuals. By educating themselves, seeking resources, and providing unconditional love and support, parents can play a significant role in empowering their child to navigate their unique gender journey with confidence and authenticity.

Supporting Genderqueer Children and Adolescents

The journey of parenting a genderqueer child or adolescent can be filled with uncertainties and questions. As a parent, it is essential to understand and support your child's unique gender identity, even if it challenges societal norms. This subchapter aims to guide parents of gender nonconforming individuals, specifically those who fall under the niche of "The Undefined Sex at Birth," on how to navigate and support their genderqueer children and adolescents.

Firstly, it is crucial to educate yourself about genderqueer identities and the experiences that your child may face. This knowledge will equip you with a better understanding of your child's feelings, struggles, and triumphs. Seek out resources, such as books, articles, and support groups, that provide insights into gender diversity and the experiences of genderqueer individuals. Understanding the terminology and language used within the genderqueer community will foster effective communication with your child.

Creating a safe and supportive environment at home is paramount. Ensure that your child feels comfortable expressing their gender identity without fear of judgment or rejection. Use gender-neutral language and pronouns when referring to your child, and encourage family members and friends to do the same. Respect your child's choices regarding clothing, hairstyles, and activities, allowing them to explore their gender expression freely.

Open and honest communication is vital in supporting a genderqueer child. Encourage your child to share their thoughts and feelings with you, and actively listen without judgment. Validate their experiences and emotions, and let them know that you love and accept them unconditionally. Be prepared for your child's gender identity to evolve over time, and be flexible and supportive throughout their journey.

Engaging with professionals who specialize in gender diversity can also be beneficial. Seek out therapists, counselors, or support groups that have experience working with genderqueer children and adolescents. These professionals can provide guidance and support for both you and your child, helping you navigate the challenges that may arise.

Finally, connect with other parents who are also supporting genderqueer children. Joining support groups or online communities can provide you with a network of individuals who understand your experiences and can offer advice and support. Sharing stories and strategies with other parents can be comforting and empowering, reminding you that you are not alone on this journey.

Supporting genderqueer children and adolescents requires love, understanding, and openness. By educating yourself, creating a safe environment, fostering communication, seeking professional support, and connecting with other parents, you can provide the support and affirmation that your genderqueer child needs to thrive in their unique gender identity.

Addressing Challenges and Promoting Acceptance

In this subchapter, we will delve into the vital aspects of addressing challenges and promoting acceptance when it comes to parenting gender nonconforming individuals, particularly those born with an undefined sex. As parents, it is essential to create a nurturing and supportive environment for your child, allowing them to explore and express their gender identity freely.

One of the primary challenges parents face is navigating societal norms and expectations. The undefined sex at birth can cause confusion and discomfort for both the child and their parents. It is crucial to educate yourself about gender diversity and the spectrum of gender identities, as this knowledge will assist you in understanding your child's experiences better. Seek out resources, such as books, online communities, and support groups, that can provide guidance and insights into parenting gender nonconforming individuals.

Open and honest communication with your child is key in addressing challenges. Encourage your child to express their feelings, thoughts, and concerns, and actively listen without judgment. Validate their experiences and let them know that their gender identity is valid and respected. By creating a safe space for open dialogue, you can help your child build self-confidence and resilience.

Another challenge parents may encounter is dealing with external discrimination and prejudice. It is crucial to prepare your child for potential negative experiences and equip them with the tools to handle such situations. Teach them about their rights, promote self-advocacy skills, and provide them with strategies to respond to discrimination. Additionally, fostering a sense of community and connecting with other parents of gender nonconforming individuals can be incredibly empowering and supportive for both you and your child.

Promoting acceptance within your family and wider social circles is essential. Educate your extended family members, friends, and community about gender diversity. Encourage them to use proper pronouns and respect your child's chosen name and gender identity. By fostering understanding and acceptance, you create a supportive network that can positively impact your child's well-being.

In conclusion, addressing challenges and promoting acceptance for parents of gender nonconforming individuals born with an undefined sex requires education, open communication, and fostering a supportive environment. By embracing your child's gender identity, advocating for their rights, and nurturing acceptance within your family and community, you can provide them with the love and support they need to navigate their unique journey. Remember, every child deserves to be celebrated and accepted for who they are, regardless of societal norms or expectations.

Chapter 7: Genderfluid Individuals

Understanding Genderfluid Identity

Genderfluid identity refers to a gender identity that is not fixed and may fluctuate over time. Individuals who identify as genderfluid may experience shifts in their gender identity, sometimes feeling more aligned with a particular gender at one time and then another gender at a different time. This fluidity can manifest in various ways, such as changes in gender expression, pronoun preferences, and even the sense of self.

For parents of individuals who identify as genderfluid, it is crucial to understand and support their child's unique journey. This subchapter aims to provide parents with insights into understanding genderfluid identity and offering guidance on how to navigate this aspect of their child's life.

Firstly, it is essential to recognize that genderfluidity is a legitimate and valid identity. It is not a phase or attention-seeking behavior. Genderfluid individuals often experience a deep sense of discomfort and dysphoria when their gender identity is not acknowledged or respected. As parents, it is crucial to provide a safe and accepting environment for your child to explore and express their gender identity freely.

Understanding genderfluidity also requires familiarizing yourself with the concept of gender as a spectrum rather than a binary. Traditionally, society has defined gender as either male or female, but this rigid categorization fails to capture the diverse range of gender identities that exist. By embracing the idea that gender exists on a continuum, parents can better comprehend their child's fluid identity and provide the necessary support.

Communication plays a vital role in navigating genderfluid identity within the family. Encourage open and honest conversations with your child about their feelings and experiences. Validate their emotions and let them know that you are there to support them unconditionally. It is essential to use the correct pronouns and gender-neutral language that your child prefers, as this demonstrates respect for their identity.

Support groups and resources can be invaluable for parents seeking guidance on how to support their genderfluid child effectively. Connecting with other parents who are navigating similar experiences can provide a sense of community and shared wisdom. Additionally, seeking out literature, educational workshops, or therapy sessions can enhance your understanding and equip you with the necessary tools to support your child.

Remember, as a parent, your role is to unconditionally love and support your child. Understanding genderfluid identity is a journey, and it is okay to make mistakes along the way. By actively seeking knowledge, fostering communication, and providing a safe space, you can help your child navigate their genderfluid identity with confidence and self-acceptance.

Nurturing a Fluid Identity in Children and Teens

In this subchapter, we will explore the importance of nurturing a fluid identity in children and teens, especially those who identify as gender nonconforming or fall under the category of "The Undefined Sex at Birth." As parents, it is crucial to create a safe and supportive environment that allows our children to explore and express their true selves.

Firstly, it is essential to understand that gender identity is not fixed and can be fluid. Many children and teens may not fit into traditional gender norms, and that is okay. By embracing and accepting their unique identities, we can help them develop a healthy sense of self-esteem and self-acceptance.

One of the most important aspects of nurturing a fluid identity is providing a space for open communication. Encourage your child to express their feelings, thoughts, and questions about their gender identity without judgment. Listening attentively and showing empathy will help your child feel validated and understood.

Educating yourself about gender diversity is another crucial step. Learn about different gender identities, terminologies, and experiences to better support your child. This knowledge will enable you to answer their questions and address any concerns they may have. Additionally, seeking out support groups or connecting with other parents facing similar situations can provide a valuable network for guidance and shared experiences.

Creating a gender-affirming environment is vital for your child's well-being. This involves respecting their chosen name and pronouns, allowing them to express themselves through clothing and hairstyles, and providing access to gender-neutral spaces. By doing so, you are showing your child that their identity is valid and worthy of celebration.

Encourage your child to explore their interests and hobbies without conforming to societal gender norms. For instance, if your child assigned female at birth enjoys playing sports traditionally associated with males, support and encourage their participation. By breaking down gender barriers and stereotypes, you are fostering their sense of empowerment and freedom to be themselves.

Lastly, be an advocate for your child within your community. Talk to educators, healthcare providers, and other influential individuals to ensure that your child's gender identity is respected and supported in all aspects of their life. Together, we can create a world that celebrates and embraces all gender identities.

Remember, nurturing a fluid identity in children and teens is a lifelong journey. By providing love, acceptance, and support, you are empowering your child to navigate their own unique path and become their authentic selves.

Fostering Empathy and Understanding in the Family

Introduction:

In a world that often categorizes individuals based on their gender, it can be challenging for parents to navigate the journey of raising a gender nonconforming child. However, fostering empathy and understanding within the family is crucial for creating a safe and supportive environment. This subchapter aims to provide practical tips and insights for parents of gender nonconforming individuals, specifically those who were assigned an undefined sex at birth.

1. Embrace Open Communication:

Creating an atmosphere of open communication is the foundation for fostering empathy and understanding within the family. Encourage your child to express their feelings, thoughts, and experiences without judgment. Regularly check in with them to understand their needs and concerns, and be prepared to actively listen and validate their emotions.

2. Educate Yourself:

To better understand your child's unique journey, take the initiative to educate yourself about gender nonconformity and the challenges faced by individuals assigned an undefined sex at birth. Read books, attend workshops, and engage with online communities to gain insights from both professionals and parents who have gone through similar experiences. Knowledge will empower you to support your child effectively.

3. Promote Empathy among Siblings:

Siblings play a vital role in a child's life, and fostering empathy among them is crucial. Encourage your children to engage in open conversations about gender and differences. Teach them to appreciate diversity and embrace their sibling's identity. By promoting empathy and understanding among siblings, you create a strong support network within the family.

4. Seek Support Networks:

Navigating the challenges of raising a gender nonconforming child can be overwhelming, but remember that you are not alone. Seek out local support groups, online forums, or counseling services specifically tailored to parents of gender nonconforming individuals with undefined sex at birth. Connecting with others who share similar experiences can provide invaluable support and guidance.

5. Encourage Self-Expression:

Allow your child the freedom to express themselves authentically, both within the family and in public. Encourage them to dress and present themselves in a way that aligns with their gender identity, even if it challenges societal norms. By validating their self-expression, you help build their confidence and reinforce the importance of self-acceptance.

Conclusion:

Fostering empathy and understanding within the family is an ongoing process, but it is essential for the well-being and happiness of gender nonconforming individuals. By embracing open communication, educating yourself, promoting empathy among siblings, seeking support networks, and encouraging self-expression, you can create a nurturing environment that allows your child to thrive. Remember, your love and understanding are the most powerful tools in helping your child navigate their unique gender journey.

Chapter 8: Agender Individuals

Exploring Agender Identity

In this subchapter, we will delve into the concept of agender identity and provide guidance for parents of gender nonconforming individuals who identify as agender. Agender individuals do not identify with any gender, feeling a lack of connection to either male or female identities. They may describe themselves as genderless, neutral, or having a gender identity that is completely detached from the traditional binary understanding of gender.

Understanding and supporting your child's agender identity can be challenging, but it is essential for their well-being and self-acceptance. Remember, you are not alone in this journey, and your love and support can make a significant difference in your child's life.

The first step in exploring your child's agender identity is to educate yourself. Learn about the different identities under the nonbinary umbrella, including agender. This knowledge will help you understand the unique experiences and challenges your child may face. It is crucial to approach this learning process with an open mind and a willingness to learn from your child's experiences.

Take the time to have open and honest conversations with your child. Ask them about their feelings and experiences, and listen attentively without judgment. Creating a safe space for them to express themselves will foster trust and strengthen your relationship. Encourage them to share their thoughts, emotions, and any challenges they may be facing.

Support groups and communities can be invaluable resources for both you and your child. Seek out local or online support groups where you can connect with other parents who have similar experiences. These groups can provide a safe and empathetic environment to share stories, seek advice, and gain insights from others who have navigated similar situations.

It is also crucial to advocate for your child's rights and well-being. Educate yourself on the legal protections and rights that exist for gender nonconforming individuals, and use this knowledge to advocate for your child's needs in schools, healthcare systems, and other institutions they interact with.

Remember, your child's journey is unique, and they may evolve in their understanding of their gender identity over time. Be patient, supportive, and willing to adapt as they explore and grow. Your acceptance and unwavering support will help them navigate the challenges they may face and thrive in a world that still has much to learn about gender diversity.

By exploring agender identity together, you can create a nurturing environment where your child can truly be themselves, free from societal expectations and constraints.

Supporting Agender Children and Adolescents

In this subchapter, we will explore the unique experiences and challenges faced by agender children and adolescents and discuss strategies for supporting their gender identity. Agender individuals do not identify with any specific gender, feeling a lack of connection to the traditional concepts of male or female. As parents of agender children, it is crucial to provide a nurturing and inclusive environment that allows them to explore and express their gender identity freely.

Understanding your child's identity is the first step towards supporting them. Take the time to educate yourself about what it means to be agender. Seek out resources, books, and online communities that offer insights into the experiences of agender individuals. This knowledge will enable you to have informed and empathetic conversations with your child about their gender identity.

Open communication is vital in supporting your agender child or adolescent. Create a safe and judgment-free space where they can express their feelings, concerns, and questions about their gender identity. Encourage discussions about gender and identity, and listen attentively without imposing your own beliefs or assumptions. Validate their experiences and offer reassurance that their feelings are valid and accepted.

Respect your child's preferred pronouns and name. Agender individuals often choose gender-neutral pronouns such as they/them or ze/zir. Make an effort to use the correct pronouns consistently and educate other family members and close friends about the importance of doing the same. Validating your child's chosen name and pronouns shows them that you accept and support their gender identity.

Connect with support networks and communities specifically designed for parents of agender children. These communities provide an invaluable opportunity to share experiences, seek advice, and learn from others who are navigating similar journeys. Engaging with these support networks can help you gain insight into the challenges faced by agender children and adolescents and discover effective strategies for supporting your child.

Advocate for your child's needs in educational and healthcare settings. Foster open and honest communication with teachers, school administrators, and healthcare providers about your child's gender identity. Work together to create inclusive policies that respect and affirm your child's gender identity, ensuring they have access to appropriate resources, support, and accommodations.

Remember, supporting your agender child or adolescent is an ongoing process that requires patience, understanding, and continuous learning. By embracing your child's gender identity, providing a supportive environment, and advocating for their needs, you play a crucial role in nurturing their self-esteem and overall well-being.

Embracing Nonconformity and Celebrating Individuality

In today's world, it is more important than ever to embrace nonconformity and celebrate individuality, especially when it comes to our children. As parents, we are often faced with the challenge of understanding and supporting our gender nonconforming children. This chapter aims to provide guidance and insights for parents of gender nonconforming individuals who fall under the category of "The Undefined Sex at Birth."

When a child's sex at birth is undefined, it can be a confusing and challenging journey for both the child and their parents. It is crucial to remember that gender is not solely determined by biological sex, but rather it is a deeply personal and individual experience. Each child deserves the freedom to explore and express their gender identity without fear or judgment.

As parents, it is essential to educate ourselves about gender diversity and the experiences of gender nonconforming individuals. By understanding the complexities of gender identity, we can better support our children on their unique journeys. This chapter will provide resources, including books, websites, and support groups, to help parents navigate this process and find a community of like-minded individuals.

One of the most important steps in supporting our gender nonconforming children is creating a safe and accepting environment at home. This means challenging societal norms and expectations surrounding gender and allowing our children to express themselves authentically. Encourage open and honest conversations about gender, and let your child know that you love and accept them unconditionally.

It is also crucial to involve your child in decision-making processes regarding their gender expression. Allow them to choose their preferred pronouns, clothing, and hairstyles. By giving them agency over their identity, you are empowering them to embrace their nonconformity and celebrate their individuality.

Navigating the journey of a gender nonconforming child can be overwhelming, but remember that you are not alone. Seek out support groups and organizations that specialize in supporting families like yours. Connect with other parents who are going through similar experiences, as their insights and understanding can be invaluable.

In conclusion, embracing nonconformity and celebrating individuality is a crucial aspect of supporting gender nonconforming children. By educating ourselves, creating a safe and accepting environment, involving our children in decision-making, and seeking support, we can navigate this journey with love and understanding. Let us embrace our children's unique identities and empower them to be proud of who they are.

Chapter 9: Bigender Individuals

Understanding Bigender Identity

In this subchapter, we will explore the concept of bigender identity and its significance for individuals who do not conform to traditional gender norms. As parents of gender nonconforming individuals, it is crucial to familiarize ourselves with diverse gender identities to better support and understand our children.

Bigender individuals identify as having two distinct gender identities, either simultaneously or at different times. These identities can be binary (male and female) or non-binary (genderqueer, genderfluid, etc.). The experience of being bigender is unique to each individual, and it is important to create a safe space for your child to express their feelings and explore their identity.

The undefined sex at birth is a term used to describe individuals whose assigned sex at birth does not align with their true gender identity. For parents of children born with an undefined sex, understanding and educating oneself about bigender identity can be particularly helpful in providing support and guidance.

When a child expresses bigender identity, it is crucial to listen and validate their experiences. Encourage open and honest communication, allowing your child to express themselves without fear of judgment or rejection. Remember, their gender identity is an intrinsic part of who they are, and it is essential to affirm and respect their self-identified gender.

It is important to educate yourself about the challenges faced by individuals with bigender identity. Take the time to research and learn about the experiences, struggles, and triumphs of bigender individuals. This knowledge will enable you to better empathize with your child and advocate for them in various environments, including schools, healthcare settings, and social interactions.

Seeking support from communities and organizations that specialize in bigender identities can provide valuable resources and connections for both you and your child. These communities can offer guidance, support groups, and workshops that will help you navigate the complexities of bigender identity.

Remember, your child's gender identity is not a phase or a choice. It is an authentic expression of who they are. By understanding and embracing their bigender identity, you can create an environment that fosters their self-acceptance, self-love, and overall well-being.

In conclusion, understanding bigender identity is essential for parents of gender nonconforming individuals. By educating yourself, listening to your child, seeking support, and creating a safe and accepting environment, you can empower your child to embrace their true selves and navigate the challenges they may face with confidence and resilience.

Navigating Dual Gender Expression and Identity

In today's society, the concept of gender is becoming more fluid and diverse, challenging traditional norms and expectations. As parents, it is important to understand and support our gender nonconforming children, particularly those who identify with dual gender expression and identity. This subchapter aims to provide guidance and insights for parents of gender nonconforming individuals who do not fit within the confines of the binary gender system, commonly referred to as "The Undefined Sex at Birth."

Gender nonconforming individuals who identify with dual gender expression and identity often feel that their experience encompasses both masculine and feminine qualities, defying societal expectations of gender roles. It is crucial for parents to create an environment of love, acceptance, and understanding, where their children can freely explore and express their unique gender identity.

First and foremost, it is important to educate ourselves about gender diversity. This will allow us to understand the nuances of dual gender expression and identity and how it may differ from other gender nonconforming experiences. Seek out resources such as books, articles, and support groups that specifically address the concerns and challenges faced by individuals who identify with dual gender expression.

In supporting our children, communication plays a vital role. Encourage open and honest conversations about their feelings and experiences. Listen to their stories without judgment, allowing them to express themselves without fear. By actively listening, we can gain valuable insights into their thoughts, emotions, and needs.

Parents should also strive to create a safe and inclusive environment for their children. This may involve challenging our own preconceived notions and biases about gender. By embracing and celebrating the uniqueness of our children's gender expression and identity, we can help them develop a strong sense of self and self-acceptance.

It is important to remember that each individual's journey is unique. As parents, we must be prepared to adapt and learn alongside our children. Seek out support groups and communities where you can connect with other parents facing similar challenges. These communities can provide a space for sharing experiences, advice, and emotional support.

In conclusion, navigating dual gender expression and identity requires a deep understanding, open communication, and unwavering support from parents. By embracing and celebrating our children's unique gender identities, we can empower them to thrive in a society that is still grappling with the concept of gender diversity. Together, let us create a world where all individuals, regardless of their gender expression, can live authentically and be embraced for who they truly are.

Encouraging Healthy Self-Acceptance and Confidence

In a society that often categorizes individuals based on their assigned sex at birth, it can be challenging for parents of gender nonconforming individuals to navigate their children's unique journeys. However, by fostering healthy self-acceptance and confidence, parents can provide a solid foundation for their children to thrive.

The Undefined Sex at Birth is a niche that encompasses parents whose children do not fit within traditional gender norms. These parents often face a multitude of questions and concerns when it comes to supporting their child's self-identity. This subchapter aims to provide guidance and strategies for encouraging healthy self-acceptance and confidence within the context of gender nonconformity.

First and foremost, it is essential for parents to create a safe and supportive environment for their child. This means actively listening to their child's feelings and experiences, validating their emotions, and assuring them that they are loved unconditionally. By doing so, parents can foster a sense of belonging and acceptance that is crucial for their child's self-esteem.

Another vital aspect of encouraging healthy self-acceptance is helping children develop a positive self-image. This can be achieved by celebrating their unique qualities and interests, regardless of societal expectations. Encourage your child to explore their passions, whether it's through art, sports, music, or any other avenue. By nurturing their talents and interests, you are instilling confidence and helping them to embrace their individuality.

Furthermore, it is important to educate yourself as a parent about gender diversity and nonconformity. Expand your knowledge on the subject, attend workshops, or join support groups specifically tailored for parents of gender nonconforming individuals. Understanding the concept of gender as a spectrum rather than a binary can help you support your child's self-discovery and affirm their identity.

Lastly, encourage open communication within your family. Create a safe space for your child to express themselves and share their thoughts and concerns. Regularly check in with them about their emotional well-being, ensuring that they feel heard and understood.

Navigating the journey of gender nonconformity can be overwhelming, but by encouraging healthy self-acceptance and confidence, parents can empower their children to embrace their true selves. Remember, your love and support are the foundations upon which your child can build a strong sense of self-worth and resilience.

Chapter 10: Two-spirit Individuals

Exploring Two-spirit Identity

In the journey of understanding and supporting your gender nonconforming child, it is crucial to explore and appreciate the diversity of gender identities that exist. One such identity is the Two-spirit identity, which has deep historical and cultural significance in many indigenous communities. This subchapter aims to shed light on the Two-spirit identity, helping parents navigate this aspect of their child's gender expression.

The term "Two-spirit" encompasses a wide range of gender identities and expressions within indigenous cultures. Traditionally, Two-spirit individuals held a revered status within their communities, often fulfilling important spiritual and ceremonial roles. They were seen as embodying both masculine and feminine qualities, and their unique perspectives were valued and respected.

Understanding and accepting Two-spirit identity requires recognizing that gender is not confined to the binary construct of male or female. Two-spirit individuals may identify as male, female, or neither, and their gender expression can vary widely. It is important for parents to create a safe and supportive environment where their child can explore and express their own Two-spirit identity without judgment or pressure to conform.

To better understand and support your child, take the time to educate yourself about the history and cultural significance of Two-spirit identity within indigenous communities. Engage in respectful conversations with indigenous individuals and organizations, seeking guidance and insights into their experiences. Remember that the experiences and perspectives of Two-spirit individuals may vary across cultures and communities, so it is essential to approach this topic with cultural sensitivity and respect.

Navigating your child's Two-spirit identity may involve challenging societal norms and preconceived ideas about gender. It is crucial to foster an open dialogue with your child, allowing them to share their feelings, thoughts, and questions. Encourage them to express themselves authentically, validating their unique identity and experiences.

As a parent, you have the opportunity to advocate for your child's Two-spirit identity within your family, community, and educational institutions. By educating others and raising awareness, you can help create a more inclusive and accepting society for all gender nonconforming individuals, including those who identify as Two-spirit.

Remember, your child's gender journey is unique, and embracing their Two-spirit identity is an integral part of their self-discovery. By exploring and celebrating the diversity of gender identities, you are fostering an environment of love, acceptance, and understanding for your child and others who may identify as Two-spirit.

In conclusion, exploring the Two-spirit identity is an important aspect of supporting your gender nonconforming child. By being open-minded, educating yourself, and fostering a safe and accepting environment, you can help your child navigate their unique gender journey with love and understanding. Embrace the beauty of diversity and celebrate your child's authentic self.

Honoring Indigenous Perspectives and Traditions

In our journey to support and understand our gender nonconforming children, it is essential that we explore and appreciate diverse perspectives and traditions. As parents, we have the responsibility to create a safe and inclusive environment for our children, and that includes recognizing and honoring the wisdom of indigenous communities.

Indigenous cultures have long held diverse understandings of gender, often recognizing more than the binary concepts that dominate mainstream society. These rich traditions offer valuable insights into the complexities of gender and can help us broaden our own perspectives.

Many indigenous cultures recognize the existence of more than two genders. They embrace the idea that gender is fluid and can encompass a wide range of expressions. Some indigenous cultures have specific terms and roles for individuals who do not fit neatly into the binary categories of male or female. By exploring these traditions, we can learn to appreciate the beauty and diversity of gender expressions.

Moreover, indigenous cultures often emphasize the interconnectedness of all living beings. This holistic perspective can guide us in supporting our gender nonconforming children. By fostering a sense of interconnectedness and respect for all forms of life, we can create a nurturing environment that embraces and celebrates our children's unique identities.

One way to honor indigenous perspectives is to engage with local indigenous communities and leaders. Seek out opportunities to learn directly from indigenous voices, whether through attending cultural events, participating in workshops, or connecting with indigenous organizations. By doing so, we can gain a deeper understanding of their traditions, histories, and perspectives on gender.

It is also important to recognize that indigenous cultures have faced immense challenges due to colonization and ongoing systemic oppression. As parents, we must actively work to dismantle these systems of power and advocate for indigenous rights. By supporting indigenous communities, we can contribute to creating a more equitable and inclusive society for all.

In conclusion, honoring indigenous perspectives and traditions is an essential part of navigating gender as parents of gender nonconforming individuals. By embracing the wisdom of indigenous cultures, we can expand our understanding of gender, celebrate diversity, and create a more inclusive environment for our children. Let us embark on this journey of learning, respect, and solidarity with indigenous communities, as we work towards a world where all gender nonconforming children can thrive.

Building Bridges of Understanding and Respect

In a rapidly evolving world, where traditional notions of gender are being challenged and redefined, it is essential for parents to navigate the complexities of raising gender nonconforming individuals. This subchapter titled "Building Bridges of Understanding and Respect" aims to provide valuable insights and guidance to parents of children who were assigned an undefined sex at birth.

Understanding the unique challenges faced by parents of gender nonconforming children is crucial to creating a supportive and nurturing environment. It is important to acknowledge that the journey of self-discovery for these individuals might be different from what society typically expects. As parents, it is our responsibility to educate ourselves and empathize with our children's experiences, even if they challenge our preconceived notions.

Building bridges of understanding begins with open and honest communication. Engage in meaningful conversations with your child, making them feel heard and valued. Encourage them to express their feelings, thoughts, and concerns, fostering a safe space where they can be their authentic selves. Remember, a child's gender identity is not a phase or a choice but an integral part of who they are.

Respect is the cornerstone of any healthy relationship. Show respect for your child's pronouns, chosen name, and gender expression. It may take time for family members and friends to adjust, but gently remind them of the importance of accepting and respecting your child's identity. Encourage open discussions to address any misconceptions or biases they may hold, helping them understand that supporting your child is essential for their overall well-being.

Seeking guidance and support from professionals, such as therapists specializing in gender nonconformity, can be immensely beneficial. These experts can help you navigate the challenges and provide strategies to foster positive self-esteem, mental health, and resilience in your child. Additionally, connecting with support groups and communities that cater to parents of gender nonconforming individuals can offer invaluable insights and a sense of belonging.

Remember that building bridges of understanding and respect is an ongoing process. Society's norms and perceptions will continue to evolve, and it is crucial to keep learning, unlearning, and adapting as parents. By nurturing a relationship of love, acceptance, and understanding, we can empower our children to embrace their true selves and navigate the world with confidence and pride.

As parents of children assigned an undefined sex at birth, we have the power to create a safer, more inclusive world for our children and future generations. Let us embark on this transformative journey together, supporting and celebrating the beautiful diversity of gender identities within our families and communities.

Chapter 11: Androgynous Individuals

Defining Androgynous Identity

In today's rapidly evolving society, traditional gender norms are being challenged, and individuals are embracing a wider range of gender identities. As parents, it is essential to educate ourselves about these diverse identities to support and understand our gender nonconforming children fully. This subchapter, "Defining Androgynous Identity," aims to shed light on this particular identity and provide guidance to parents navigating through this journey.

Androgynous individuals are those who identify with both masculine and feminine qualities, blurring the lines between traditional gender stereotypes. They may reject the idea of conforming to societal expectations of gender expression and instead embrace a fluid and balanced combination of both masculine and feminine attributes. It is important to note that androgyny is a unique and personal experience, and each individual may express it differently.

Parents of children assigned an undefined sex at birth face distinct challenges when it comes to understanding their child's gender identity. These children may not fit neatly into the categories of male or female, leading to confusion and uncertainty. This subchapter aims to provide support and guidance to parents navigating this uncharted territory.

Understanding and embracing an androgynous identity is crucial for parents to foster an inclusive and supportive environment for their children. By acknowledging and validating their child's unique expression, parents can help them develop a strong sense of self and self-acceptance. It is essential to create an open and non-judgmental space for dialogue, allowing for discussions about gender identity and expression.

Parents should also familiarize themselves with gender-neutral pronouns and language, as these are important tools for affirming and validating their child's androgynous identity. By using the correct pronouns and language, parents demonstrate their support and respect for their child's self-identified gender.

It is also important to recognize that androgynous individuals may face challenges in a society that often favors binary gender classifications. Parents can play a vital role in advocating for their child's rights and creating safe spaces for them to express themselves authentically. This may involve educating others, such as extended family members, friends, and school administrators, about the importance of using inclusive language and respecting their child's gender identity.

In conclusion, understanding and supporting an androgynous identity is a critical aspect of parenting gender nonconforming children assigned an undefined sex at birth. By embracing their child's unique expression, using inclusive language, and advocating for their rights, parents can create a nurturing and accepting environment that allows their child to thrive.

Supporting Androgynous Children and Teens

In today's diverse and ever-evolving world, it is crucial for parents to embrace and support their children's gender expressions, even if it challenges societal norms. This subchapter aims to provide guidance and insights into supporting androgynous children and teens, those who do not conform to traditional gender expectations and identify beyond the binary.

Understanding Androgyny

To begin, it is essential to understand what androgyny means. Androgyny refers to individuals who exhibit characteristics or behaviors that are not exclusively masculine or feminine. These children may express themselves in ways that encompass a blend of both genders or refuse to adhere to conventional gender roles altogether. Acknowledging and embracing their unique identity is key to fostering a healthy and supportive environment.

Acceptance and Open Communication

As parents, the first step towards supporting androgynous children and teens is accepting their gender identity. By creating an atmosphere of acceptance and love, parents can empower their children to express themselves authentically. Engaging in open and honest communication is vital. Encourage your child to share their feelings and experiences, and actively listen without judgment.

Education and Advocacy

Educating yourself about gender diversity is crucial in providing the necessary support for your child. Expand your knowledge by reading books, attending workshops, or joining support groups. By becoming an advocate for your child, you can challenge societal misconceptions and promote inclusivity. Advocate for gender-neutral policies in schools, encourage teachers to address students by their preferred pronouns, and support the creation of safe spaces for gender nonconforming individuals.

Respecting Personal Choices

Respecting your child's personal choices is paramount. Allow them the freedom to express themselves through clothing, hairstyle, and hobbies without imposing your own expectations. Encourage them to explore their interests and provide them with opportunities to discover their true selves.

Building a Support Network

Building a support network for your child is essential. Seek out organizations, therapists, or support groups that specialize in gender diversity. Connecting with other parents who have similar experiences can provide a safe space to share challenges and successes. Remember, you are not alone in this journey, and building a community can help both you and your child navigate the complexities of gender nonconformity.

In conclusion, supporting androgynous children and teens requires acceptance, open communication, education, advocacy, and respect for personal choices. By embracing their unique gender identities and providing a supportive environment, parents can empower their children to thrive confidently in a world that too often adheres to strict gender norms. Remember, your child's happiness and well-being should always be the priority, and by navigating this journey together, you can create a brighter and more inclusive future for them.

Challenging Gender Stereotypes and Promoting Authenticity

In today's society, it is becoming increasingly important to challenge traditional gender stereotypes and promote authenticity among individuals, particularly those who identify as gender nonconforming. As parents, it is our responsibility to support and guide our children, regardless of the sex they were assigned at birth, as they navigate their gender identity.

The Undefined Sex at Birth is a complex and delicate situation that requires a deep understanding and acceptance from parents. It is crucial to acknowledge that gender is not solely determined by biological factors, but rather a deeply personal and individual experience. By challenging societal norms and embracing authenticity, we can create a safe and nurturing environment for our children to explore their gender identity without fear of judgment or rejection.

One of the first steps in challenging gender stereotypes is to educate ourselves about the various gender identities and expressions that exist beyond the binary. By expanding our knowledge and understanding, we can better support our children in their journey of self-discovery. This may involve seeking out resources, attending support groups, or connecting with other parents who have faced similar situations.

As parents, it is essential to communicate openly with our children and create a space where they feel comfortable expressing their true selves. Encourage open dialogue and listen attentively to their thoughts and feelings. Validate their experiences and emotions, even if they may differ from our own preconceived notions or societal expectations.

Promoting authenticity involves allowing our children to explore and experiment with their gender expression. Encourage them to dress and present themselves in a way that aligns with their true identity, even if it challenges traditional norms. Advocate for their autonomy and ensure they have access to clothing, toys, and activities that align with their self-expression.

It is also important to address any internalized biases or fears we may have as parents. Understand that our own upbringing and societal conditioning might influence our initial reactions or concerns. By acknowledging and challenging these biases, we can better support our children in their journey towards self-acceptance.

Navigating the undefined sex at birth can be a challenging and emotional journey for both parents and their gender nonconforming children. However, by challenging gender stereotypes and promoting authenticity, we can create a world that celebrates diversity and empowers individuals to embrace their true selves. Together, let us be the guiding light for our children, ensuring they feel loved, supported, and accepted every step of the way.

Chapter 12: Nurturing an Inclusive Family Environment

Open Communication and Active Listening

In the journey of understanding and supporting gender nonconforming individuals, one of the most vital tools that parents can possess is open communication and active listening. By creating a safe and nurturing environment where your child feels comfortable expressing themselves, you can foster a strong bond built on trust, love, and acceptance.

For parents of children with an undefined sex at birth, it is crucial to approach conversations about gender with an open mind. Your child may not fit neatly into societal expectations, and it is essential to embrace their uniqueness. Encourage them to explore their gender identity and provide a judgment-free space for them to share their thoughts and feelings.

Gender nonconforming individuals face unique challenges in a world that often adheres to binary gender norms. As a parent, it is crucial to actively listen to your child's experiences and emotions. By affirming their identity and validating their feelings, you can help them navigate the complexities they may encounter.

Intersex individuals may have a complex relationship with gender due to their biological differences. Open communication is key in understanding their experiences and ensuring they feel supported in their journey. By actively listening and seeking guidance from medical professionals, you can provide the necessary resources and support they need.

For parents of non-binary individuals, transgender individuals, genderqueer individuals, genderfluid individuals, agender individuals, bigender individuals, two-spirit individuals, androgynous individuals, it is crucial to have ongoing conversations about their gender identity. Actively listen to their preferences and pronouns, and respect their self-identified gender expression. Create an environment where they feel comfortable expressing themselves openly and without fear of judgment.

Open communication and active listening are fundamental in building trust and maintaining a strong parent-child relationship. Remember, your child's journey is unique, and by fostering an open and accepting atmosphere, you can provide the support they need to thrive.

In conclusion, open communication and active listening are invaluable tools for parents of gender nonconforming individuals. By creating a safe and nonjudgmental space, you can foster a strong bond with your child and support them in their journey of self-discovery. Whether your child identifies as non-binary, transgender, genderqueer, genderfluid, agender, bigender, two-spirit, androgynous, or has an undefined sex at birth, actively listening to their experiences and affirming their identity will help them navigate the complexities of gender with confidence and resilience.

Educating Extended Family and Friends

As parents of gender nonconforming individuals, it is not only crucial to support and understand our own children, but also to educate our extended family and friends. This subchapter aims to provide guidance and strategies for navigating the sometimes challenging task of educating those around us.

First and foremost, it is important to approach these conversations with empathy and understanding. Remember that your extended family and friends may not have had previous exposure to the concepts of gender nonconformity or the diverse range of gender identities. Be patient and open-minded as you introduce these ideas to them.

One effective strategy is to provide resources and educational materials. Offer books, articles, or websites that explain the experiences and struggles of gender nonconforming individuals. These resources can help your loved ones gain a deeper understanding of the complexities of gender identity and the importance of acceptance.

Personal stories can also be powerful tools for education. Encourage your child to share their own experiences and feelings with your extended family and friends. Hearing firsthand accounts can help challenge preconceived notions and foster empathy.

In addition, consider organizing family gatherings or events centered around learning and discussion. Create a safe space where everyone can openly ask questions and have open conversations about gender identity. This not only allows for education but also helps build a supportive network for your child and your family.

It is important to address any concerns or misconceptions that your extended family and friends may have. Provide them with accurate information and dispel common myths or stereotypes. Encourage them to ask questions and express their concerns openly, as long as it is done respectfully and with the intention to learn.

Lastly, remember that change takes time. It may be unrealistic to expect immediate acceptance and understanding from everyone. Some family members and friends may need more time to process and adjust to these new concepts. Stay patient, continue to provide support and education, and hope for progress over time.

By educating our extended family and friends, we can create a more inclusive and supportive environment for our gender nonconforming children. Together, we can break down barriers, challenge stereotypes, and promote acceptance and love for all individuals, regardless of their gender identity.

Advocating for Inclusivity in Schools and Communities

In today's ever-evolving society, it is crucial for parents to understand the importance of advocating for inclusivity in schools and communities. As parents, we play a critical role in ensuring that our children, regardless of their gender identity or expression, have a safe and supportive environment to thrive in. This subchapter aims to provide guidance on how to advocate for inclusivity and create positive change within educational institutions and wider communities.

The Undefined Sex at Birth, Gender nonconforming individuals, Intersex individuals, Non-binary individuals, Transgender individuals, Genderqueer individuals, Genderfluid individuals, Agender individuals, Bigender individuals, Two-spirit individuals, Androgynous individuals – these are just a few of the diverse identities that our children may identify with. It is essential for us to recognize and embrace this diversity, fostering an environment that celebrates and respects the uniqueness of each individual.

One of the first steps in advocating for inclusivity is education. As parents, we must educate ourselves about gender diversity, understanding the spectrum of identities and the challenges that our children may face. By staying informed, we can effectively advocate for their rights and needs within educational institutions and community spaces.

Communication is key when advocating for inclusivity. Engage in open and honest conversations with your child's school administration, teachers, and other parents to raise awareness about the importance of creating an inclusive environment. Share resources, such as books and articles, that promote understanding and acceptance of gender diversity.

Encourage your child's school to implement inclusive policies and practices that address gender identity and expression. This could include gender-neutral restrooms, inclusive dress codes, and comprehensive anti-bullying policies. By advocating for these changes, we can ensure that our children are able to express their true selves without fear of discrimination or harassment.

Community involvement is another powerful tool for promoting inclusivity. Engage with local organizations that support gender nonconforming individuals and their families. Attend events, workshops, and support groups to connect with other parents who share similar experiences. Together, we can create a united front for inclusivity and work towards eliminating stigma and discrimination.

In conclusion, advocating for inclusivity in schools and communities is a vital responsibility for parents of gender nonconforming individuals. By educating ourselves, communicating effectively, and engaging with our communities, we can pave the way for a more accepting and inclusive society. Let us stand together, embracing the diversity of our children and ensuring that their voices are heard and respected.

Chapter 13: Resources for Parents

Books and Literature

In a world filled with diverse identities and experiences, books and literature serve as powerful tools for understanding and navigating the complexities of gender. Whether you are a parent of a gender nonconforming, intersex, non-binary, transgender, genderqueer, genderfluid, agender, bigender, two-spirit, or androgynous individual, exploring the vast realm of books and literature can be an invaluable resource for both you and your child.

Books provide a safe space for individuals to see themselves reflected, to feel understood, and to gain insight into their own identities. They offer opportunities for conversations, education, and growth within families. By incorporating books and literature into your journey, you can create an environment that fosters understanding, acceptance, and love.

For parents of gender nonconforming individuals, books like "The Gender Creative Child" by Diane Ehrensaft can guide you through the challenges and triumphs of raising a child who defies societal norms. "Raising My Rainbow" by Lori Duron is another informative and heartfelt memoir that chronicles a mother's journey of raising a gender nonconforming son.

Intersex individuals and their families can benefit from books like "Intersex (For Lack of a Better Word)" by Thea Hillman, which sheds light on the experiences and struggles faced by intersex individuals in a society that often tries to fit everyone into binary boxes.

To better understand the experiences of non-binary individuals, books such as "Beyond the Gender Binary" by Alok Vaid-Menon can provide valuable insights. "Gender Outlaws: The Next Generation" edited by Kate Bornstein and S. Bear Bergman is an anthology featuring personal stories of transgender and genderqueer individuals, offering a diverse range of perspectives.

For parents seeking guidance on supporting their transgender children, books like "The Transgender Child: A Handbook for Families and Professionals" by Stephanie Brill and Rachel Pepper can be an invaluable resource. "Becoming Nicole" by Amy Ellis Nutt is a powerful memoir that tells the story of a transgender girl and her supportive family.

Regardless of your child's gender identity, books like "They, She, He, Me: Free to Be!" by Maya Christina Gonzalez and "Who Are You? The Kid's Guide to Gender Identity" by Brook Pessin-Whedbee can help foster understanding and inclusivity, encouraging children to embrace their authentic selves.

Remember, books and literature are just one piece of the puzzle. Open and honest communication, seeking support from communities and professionals, and embracing your child's journey are equally important. Together, we can create a world that celebrates and respects all gender identities.

Support Groups and Organizations

Finding support and understanding can be crucial when navigating the journey of parenting a gender nonconforming individual. This subchapter explores the various support groups and organizations available to parents who want to connect with others who have similar experiences and concerns. These groups can provide a sense of community, guidance, and resources to help parents better understand and support their children.

The Undefined Sex at Birth

For parents whose children were born with an undefined sex, finding support can be particularly challenging. However, there are organizations that cater specifically to this group, offering guidance and support to parents navigating the complexities of raising a child with an undefined sex. These organizations can provide valuable insights and resources to help parents make informed decisions and provide a nurturing environment for their child.

Gender Nonconforming Individuals

Support groups and organizations dedicated to gender nonconforming individuals can offer parents a space to share experiences, ask questions, and learn from others who have faced similar challenges. These groups typically provide a supportive community where parents can gain knowledge, understanding, and strategies for how to support and advocate for their child in various settings, including schools, healthcare systems, and social environments.

Intersex Individuals

Parents of intersex children can benefit greatly from connecting with support groups and organizations that focus on intersex rights and advocacy. These groups can provide information about intersex conditions, medical choices, and support networks for both parents and their children. They can also offer guidance on navigating legal and medical systems, helping parents ensure their child receives compassionate and appropriate care.

Non-binary, Transgender, Genderqueer, Genderfluid, Agender, Bigender, Two-spirit, Androgynous Individuals

Parents of children who identify as non-binary, transgender, genderqueer, genderfluid, agender, bigender, two-spirit, or androgynous can find solace in support groups and organizations that cater to these specific identities. These groups often provide educational resources, counseling services, and opportunities for parents to connect with others who have firsthand experience in raising children with these identities.

They can serve as a source of strength, knowledge, and guidance for parents trying to navigate the unique challenges that come with supporting and affirming their child's gender identity.

In conclusion, support groups and organizations play a vital role in the lives of parents raising gender nonconforming individuals. Whether it is connecting with others who have children with an undefined sex, seeking guidance on intersex matters, or finding support for specific gender identities, these groups offer a safe space for parents to share their experiences and learn from others. By connecting with these support networks, parents can gain valuable insights and resources to navigate the complexities of raising their gender nonconforming child with confidence and love.

Online Platforms and Communities

In today's digital age, online platforms and communities have become powerful tools for connecting individuals from all walks of life. For parents of gender nonconforming individuals, these online spaces can be invaluable sources of support, information, and solidarity. In this subchapter, we will explore the significance of online platforms and communities in the journey of understanding and navigating gender.

The Undefined Sex at Birth:

Parents of children with an undefined sex at birth often find themselves in uncharted territory. Online platforms provide a safe space to connect with others facing similar experiences, seek guidance from experts, and share personal stories. These communities offer a sense of validation and help parents gain a better understanding of their child's unique gender identity.

Gender Nonconforming Individuals:

For parents of gender nonconforming children, finding acceptance and support from society can be challenging. Online platforms provide a refuge where parents can connect with others who have walked a similar path. These communities foster a sense of belonging and offer practical advice on how to navigate the complexities of raising a gender nonconforming child.

Intersex Individuals:

Intersex individuals and their families often face complex medical, ethical, and social challenges. Online platforms cater specifically to the needs of intersex individuals, providing a space for parents to connect with others who can offer guidance, share resources, and advocate for intersex rights. These communities empower parents to become better advocates for their children's unique needs.

Non-binary, Transgender, Genderqueer, Genderfluid, Agender, Bigender, Two-spirit, Androgynous Individuals:

Online platforms play a crucial role in creating a sense of community and support for individuals who identify as non-binary, transgender, genderqueer, genderfluid, agender, bigender, two-spirit, or androgynous. Parents can connect with other families, gain insights into their child's experiences, and access resources to help them navigate the complexities of gender identity.

These online communities offer a wealth of information on topics such as legal rights, healthcare, mental health support, and educational resources. They also provide opportunities for parents to engage in discussions, ask questions, and share their own experiences.

It is important for parents to approach online platforms and communities with caution, as not all sources may be reliable or supportive. However, with careful research and vetting, these online spaces can provide invaluable support and guidance for parents of gender nonconforming individuals.

In conclusion, online platforms and communities have revolutionized the way parents of gender nonconforming individuals connect, learn, and advocate for their children. These spaces offer a sense of community, support, and empowerment, allowing parents to navigate the complexities of gender with confidence and understanding.

Chapter 14: The Journey Continues

Celebrating Personal Growth and Learning

In the journey of parenting a gender nonconforming individual, it is crucial to recognize and celebrate personal growth and learning. This subchapter aims to remind parents of the diverse experiences and identities within the gender nonconforming community, including those of the Undefined Sex at Birth, Intersex individuals, Non-binary individuals, Transgender individuals, Genderqueer individuals, Genderfluid individuals, Agender individuals, Bigender individuals, Two-spirit individuals, Androgynous individuals, and more. By acknowledging the unique challenges and triumphs faced by each individual, parents can foster a nurturing and inclusive environment that supports personal growth and learning.

When a child expresses their gender identity, it is an opportunity for parents to embark on their own journey of learning and growth. It is essential to educate ourselves about the various gender identities and expressions, understanding that they exist on a spectrum rather than within a binary framework. By doing so, parents can better support their child's exploration and self-discovery, while also challenging societal norms and expectations.

Celebrating personal growth involves creating spaces that encourage self-expression and autonomy. Parents can engage in open and honest conversations with their children, actively listening to their experiences and allowing them to shape their own gender identity. This includes respecting their preferred pronouns, names, and clothing choices, as well as advocating for their rights within schools and communities.

As parents, it is natural to have questions and concerns. Seeking out support networks within the gender nonconforming community can provide valuable guidance and reassurance. Connecting with other parents who share similar experiences can foster a sense of solidarity and provide a platform for sharing knowledge and resources.

Furthermore, personal growth and learning should extend beyond the immediate family unit. Engaging with organizations, workshops, and conferences that focus on gender diversity can deepen our understanding of the challenges faced by our children, while also equipping us with the necessary tools to advocate for their rights.

In conclusion, celebrating personal growth and learning is an ongoing process in the journey of parenting gender nonconforming individuals. By embracing the uniqueness of each individual's gender identity and expression, parents can create an environment that fosters personal growth, self-acceptance, and resilience. Together, let us celebrate the triumphs, navigate the challenges, and continue to learn from our children, ensuring that they have the love, support, and resources they need to thrive.

Embracing Change and Resilience

In this subchapter, we will delve into the importance of embracing change and building resilience when parenting gender nonconforming individuals. Navigating the complexities of gender identity can be challenging, but by adopting a mindset of acceptance and adaptability, parents can provide a nurturing environment for their children to thrive.

The Undefined Sex at Birth

For parents whose children were assigned an undefined sex at birth, it is crucial to approach their gender exploration with an open mind. Instead of imposing societal expectations, allow your child the freedom to explore their own identity. Embrace the uncertainty and support them in discovering their authentic selves.

Gender Nonconforming Individuals

Parents of gender nonconforming individuals often face unique challenges. It is vital to create a safe and inclusive space where your child can express themselves without fear of judgment. Encourage open communication and actively educate yourself on gender diversity to better understand and support your child's journey.

Intersex Individuals

Parents of intersex individuals should prioritize open and honest conversations about their child's physical differences and unique experiences. Embrace the opportunity to learn about intersexuality and advocate for your child's rights and well-being. Seek support from intersex organizations and connect with other families who share similar experiences.

Non-binary Individuals

For parents of non-binary individuals, it is crucial to respect and affirm your child's gender identity. Educate yourself on non-binary experiences and pronouns, and encourage others to do the same. Embrace their unique journey and provide a safe space for self-discovery and expression.

Transgender Individuals

Parents of transgender individuals play a pivotal role in their child's transition. Show unwavering support, validate their identity, and seek professional guidance where necessary. Educate yourself on the medical, legal, and social aspects of transgender experiences, and connect with support networks to navigate this transformative journey together.

Genderqueer, Genderfluid, Agender, Bigender, Two-spirit, Androgynous Individuals

These diverse gender identities can be both beautiful and complex. Parents should embrace the unique experiences and expressions of their children. Encourage open dialogue, validate their identities, and advocate for their rights. Connect with communities and resources that can provide guidance and support.

Building Resilience

As parents, it is essential to help your children develop resilience in the face of adversity. Encourage self-empowerment, self-care, and self-acceptance. Teach them to navigate social challenges and equip them with the tools to advocate for themselves. Celebrate their strengths and instill in them a sense of pride in their identity.

In conclusion, embracing change and building resilience are crucial for parents of gender nonconforming individuals. By fostering open communication, educating ourselves, and providing unwavering support, we can create a nurturing environment where our children can thrive. Remember, love and acceptance are the cornerstones of this journey, and together we can navigate the complexities of gender identity with grace and strength.

Continuing to Support and Advocate for Gender Nonconforming Individuals

Supporting and advocating for gender nonconforming individuals is an ongoing journey that requires understanding, empathy, and a commitment to creating an inclusive and affirming environment for all. As parents of gender nonconforming individuals, you play a vital role in their journey of self-discovery and acceptance. This subchapter will explore various ways in which you can continue supporting and advocating for your child, as well as the broader gender nonconforming community.

1. Education and Awareness: Continue educating yourself about different gender identities and expressions. Stay updated on the latest research, terminology, and experiences of gender nonconforming individuals. This knowledge will not only help you better understand your child but also enable you to educate others and challenge misconceptions.

2. Creating Safe Spaces: Foster an environment at home where your child feels safe and supported. Encourage open communication, actively listen to their experiences, and validate their feelings. Let them know that their gender identity is valid and that you love and accept them unconditionally.

3. Community Involvement: Seek out local support groups, organizations, and events that cater to gender nonconforming individuals and their families. Connect with other parents who are on a similar journey. Sharing experiences and resources can provide a sense of belonging and support.

4. Advocacy: Take an active role in advocating for the rights and inclusion of gender nonconforming individuals. Attend workshops, conferences, and community meetings to learn about current issues and how you can contribute to positive change. Raise awareness by sharing your story and experiences with others.

5. Mental Health Support: Recognize that your child may face unique challenges related to their gender identity. Seek professional help from therapists or counselors who specialize in working with gender nonconforming individuals. Encourage your child to express their emotions and provide them with the necessary resources to maintain their mental well-being.

6. Celebrate Diversity: Embrace and celebrate the diversity within the gender nonconforming community. Encourage your child to explore

different identities and expressions without judgment. Respect their choices and help them navigate societal expectations and stereotypes.

7. Self-Care: Remember to prioritize your own well-being as a parent. Supporting a gender nonconforming child can be emotionally challenging at times. Seek support from friends, family, or support groups to ensure you have the necessary strength and resilience to continue advocating for your child.

By continuing to support and advocate for gender nonconforming individuals, you are not only helping your child thrive but also contributing to a more inclusive and accepting society. Your dedication and commitment are crucial in creating a world where all individuals, regardless of their gender identity, can live authentically and without fear.